ALL THINGS FLOW

**For Joan Maxwell,
who sparked my love for poetry
&
Roger Sworder,
who taught me its value.**

Published in 2019
by BIRDFISH BOOKS
www.birdfishbooks.com.au

The Inter-web has been published
in Plumwood Mountain.

All rights reserved. No part of this edition
of this text may be reproduced or transmitted
in any form or by any means, electronic
or mechanical, including photocopy, recording
or any informational storage and retrieval system,
without prior permission from the publisher.

Cover images: *A Seed for the Sun*, by the author
& *Impressionist Enchantment,* by Kinsey Barnard

ISBN-13: 978-0-9953718-2-8

ALL THINGS FLOW

Tegan Gigante

Pieces	7
Noumena, Phenomena	8
A Third Arena	10
The Inter-web	11
Signs of Use	14
The Short Days	15
Home	16
The Company of Trees	17
Storm Herald	18
Judgement	19
Nomine Padre	20
The Wolf	21
Pastoral / Pastoral II	22
The Mountain	24
Day River	25
Confluence	26
Avatar	27
Indigenous Installation	28

The Plane Tree	30
Forest/ry	32
Mooloort Plains, 42°	34
Big Plans for Baringhup	35
The Boys' Club	37
The Dishes	39
An Armful	42
Hungry Ghost	44
Who Down on the Heart's Rug	45
Fever Dream	47
I Will not Fall Again	46
Elemental	50
Collier's Lilith	52
The Poem	53
Strangers in the Dark	55
Time and Eternity	57
Panta Rhei	58

Pieces

Some days
there are no poems.
Only words
broken into pieces,
mouthfuls of air.
My wet tongue
considers these fragments

while I wonder whence they came
to trouble the bright afternoon;
and whether they trace a path
to redemption.

Do they desire a body
in which to suffer a brief life?
Some company
among a scattered constellation —
or silence,
to be left alone as solitary stars?

Today began
as one of those days,
empty of poetry,
until those isolated scraps
led me here.

I have not found
what I expected.

Noumena, Phenomena

I.

Whiter than clouds,
cockatoos flash wing-beat signals.
Crickets reach and hold their pitch.
The air carries eucalypt and dust.

These are the real.
There is the solid ground
on which my life rests,
the facts that allow thought to flit
and flicker in my mind's hollow drum.

I turn and reel and rush,
but when I slow to hear and see —
there are the birds,
the click of insects in the grass,
the wide and constant sky.

II.

Lighter than clouds,
thoughts flash wing-beat signals.
Dreams hold and reach out their signs.
The mind's void carries the world.

This is the real.
Here is the space
in which the sky rests,
the rarefied face of the deep
that allows solidity to enter.

I see and hear and touch,
but when I close those bright doors —
here is this hollow,
the click of knowledge in its drum,
the wide eternal inner eye.

A Third Arena

I easily image clouds as three-dimensional stories
— that rarely foretell rain over these flat lands,
where no jagged peaks may snatch at their cotton.

They reach down to us, meet our imagination
in a third arena between us and heaven,
sky dwellers swollen with our own symbols.

I blink and see stars as eyes that watch our lives
from a distant past, knowing more than we do,
predicting the circuits of our transformations.

Their paths steer the wise home to their cradles,
drawing patterns in their course across our ceiling
to reveal an order seen so precisely from earth.

And I am made to meet the moon in its chamber,
to turn as the light changes from empty to whole,
my body called by the tidal pull of a lunar pulse.

So close, so easily mirrored by my meanings,
I am swallowed by the cup of shadow that grows
as reason's light ebbs, making room for dreams.

The Inter-web

Inspecting the nectarine tree
beside the front gate
I discover green new-born leaves.
The blossoms have almost all fallen;
their brief burst of cocktail pink
now carpets the mulch beneath.
Already I miss their decoration,
though the turning season heralds fruit.

The following day,
I notice the leaf-curl:
fire-coloured convolutions
that threaten the promised crop.
Plucking the twisted leaves
I am briefly sorry to deny
this fungal claim to life.

The next time
I pay close attention to the tree,
the leaves have grown full —
so has the disease — and now,
the branches host clusters of aphid families.
Another breach of national security.
I tweezer a few between my fingers
in ineffectual spite.

Later, I spy ladybirds
feasting on the aphids,
methodically consuming
the tiny insects.

I have taken sides.

The web continues to expand.
There is now a stream of ants
snaking up the branches,
neutral agents
that depend on tree and aphid
while harming neither.
They drink the sweet gems
of clear, bright faeces
as it emerges from the nesting aphids,
and fend off hungry ladybirds in return.

The aphids need the tree
and the ants who protect them;
ladybird and ant
depend on both aphid and tree;
the fungi eats the tree,
and isn't much bothered about anyone else.
The tree depends on me
to water, feed and mulch,
and I need the tree to fruit —
no leaf-curl, no aphid, no ladybird, no ant.

But this is not a closed loop:
I watch the ants delve
into their hidden home,
networks beneath my feet
and beyond my vision.
I can no more enter their nest
than see a boundary
where the tree might end.

Signs of Use

Life coils in my palm,
slips through fingers like an eel,
leaving sly traces:

an ancestral trail,
something dark under my nails;
memories of home.

It is entrancing,
watching these signs of passage
appear on my hands:

new constellations,
liver spots and curving scars;
grooved webs of use.

I become porous,
pores in my skin opening,
breathing in the world

The Short Days

Today: weeks after mid-winter,
months before the pending spring
brings back the length of days
and winds the evening clock long
again. My life seems short
beside buds setting on the plum,
their slow stasis, patience to wait
while leaves bide inside the tree.

Grey days and rain, green flush
on the slopes, water slugging,
merging pools, streaming
to empty their full-soaked wet
into gathering rivers: sharp cold
but so alive, running in veins
shaped as my own but vast
and ancient. While the sun
waits for its due return,
the ground and I
drink our fill.

Home

The cat watches me drive away,
meets me at the door on my return.

Coming and going, home is my refuge,
a den, dipped into between days spent
elsewhere, navigating the complex maps
of my world. I piece a patchwork of space,
towns and addresses stitched by road-lines.

She extends the borders of her explorations,
finds the limits of boundary and distance
by each padding paw. Home is the centre
of a known landscape, identified upwards
from the deep scent at earth's level
to the taste of a bird's ripe heart.

I am stretched between so many nodes,
the beads of my life strewn and strung wide.
The hooks of my heart pull me to scatter,
while my animal other finds the deep shade
beneath the pines that shelter the house;
holding a centre,
a place to keep returning to;
a home where our worlds converge.

The Company of Trees

I left the house alone today
to wander in my solitude
along the dry and stony ways
that never interrupt my mood.

To wander in my solitude
I sought the company of trees
that never interrupt my mood,
but share my solitude with me.

I sought the company of trees
that keep the silence for my thoughts
but share their solitude with me
so I was not lonely as I walked.

Keeping silence for my thoughts
along the dry and stony ways
I was not lonely as I walked
though I left the house alone today.

Storm Herald

Wind tunnels through the valley,
silent, but bringing all to noise,

becoming ghosts in the chimney,
speaking through eaves and cracks,

rushing over straining saplings,
whipping leaves into ecstatic dance,

pushing every stem to test its strength —
while inside, my page does not stir

and my warm room is more calm
for the force of the storm outside.

Judgement

The star is still. Occupies the centre
around which we writhe, never still.

Watches, or does not watch, the pain
that drives our turning towards bliss.

The seat is empty. It does not judge
our revolutions, nor keep our laws.

No good or ill is kept inside the core,
where those twins converge and die.

All direction ceases here. No upwards
motion can be taken, no fall from grace.

The planet spins. So it seems the star
sets or climbs: yet only we might rise.

Light swallows dark. Time holds us fast
in our waiting, running, hoping, loving.

The stillness of the star is true. Above
the blue illusion, night is one with day.

On the ground, days and nights are true.
Left and right are real as mortal wrong.

No choices can be made within a star.
Singularity voids morality. All is well.

Nomine Padre

You write your name on my cells,
an automatic signature
replicating formulas of seed

I embody your spark of being,
your ancestral shadows,
prescriptions and proscriptions

Approval and disapproval,
all that is impossible for me to do
chipped into my stone

You handed me this tongue,
these letters and words,
chromosomes that still insist their script

I write now what I may
in handwriting almost your own,
speaking a poetry you did not intend

Writing and being written,
all that is possible for me to do
growing from a seed into a story

The Wolf
after Ted Hughes' 'Wolfwatching'

It has entered me, this wolf,
by stealth, under the old guise
of yellow-papered second-hand sight;
let in by the lapse of my usual guards,
soothed by soft late-night bedside
page-turns and light looks.

I thought to watch from a distance —
he lured my gaze, promised
a fence between his lean strength
and my fragile body —
now he has closed the distance.

The poem has left the sure muscles
of a thing, out there, to find a den
deep in the nerves that tangle
between eyes and the hot-bed of feeling,
housed somehow in the shadowlands
beneath my skull and skin.

I know he will not leave,
this beast, the new animal
will never be released;
though I may forget
he's there.

Pastoral

A white shape
in the twilit field:
a pastoral vision
that conjures a past
still haloed by myth,

an apparition wandered
from some golden age
to nose my back fence —
this perfect white calf
a revelation.

He starts with interest,
and his mother steps closer
into the landscape
to say: *I have noticed you.*
I say, *I have noticed too*

gentle dark mother,
protective of your miracle,
moving in the still mist
that settles on my hair,
diffuses the day's last light.

The cow, cautious yet calm,
unhurried, ambles away
and the white calf,
excited, kicks its heels,
dances in joyous play.

Pastoral II

In a twilit field
a white calf dances with joy —
his mother watchful.

The Mountain
for my comrades on the Falls Creek expedition, 2015

Not without risk do we stray beyond the town,
find our way past its boundaries:
poets and dreamers breaking across the wall
to brace the undefined refuge of space,
to be graced by open sky.

Not without fear have we pressed our backs
into this long march, set our feet towards life
as it calls us away from home, into itself;
as it waits, laid open like a woman in love
who might yet leave us broken, or lost.

Not without hope in our hearts do we fly,
rising with each breath to the cold
that rings the clouds, ices our intentions
to breach the atmosphere. We know
there is treasure in the labyrinth below.

And not without ache in our whole selves —
at times too much to bear
though somehow we all, in our way, bear it
nonetheless — do we sing to each other
of the great world that has called us
into itself, away from home.

Day River

The surface is busy with sunlight,
opens easily to our heat-blooded bodies:
flesh finding night's den beneath
and kissing its cold with dimpled skin.

I watch your back disappear.
Your shape does not flinch
from the river's cool touch
and steady strides belie
the mud shifting underfoot.

We find each other in the centre,
wet skins meeting under water,
becoming warmer;
the embrace stirring the surface,
chasing our movements to the edge.

Our gestures echo in the light
on wading saplings, wrapping the river
in a play of dappled shade.
Muscle to ripple to marbled reflection:
we are painting the day.

Confluence

The creek wanders south to find the river.
The road carries my car northwards, beside water
that releases cold in slow up-draughts of mist —
morning sun heating the surface, low in the valley —
night and day making steam where they meet.

I rush as the creek ambles, too late for work
to slow and savour this early light's communion.
Flashing past the fork where our paths diverge —
one to the stream's source, one taking me to town —
the trees step back, reveal an angel on the water.

A white-faced heron greets the sun,
haloed wings held open to catch its warmth.
I am carried through the whole day by its image —
those outstretched wings, that still bird —
poised in a stretched moment of the sun's rising.

Avatar

I saw an eagle, like a god
come down to ground,
dropped to earth
not to grace us
but to eat,
shredding meat
on a dry, stripped, stretch of grass
bitten low by cows
who do not raise
even one wet mouth
to the power there beside them.

Indigenous Installation
*in response to a collection of creation spirit sculptures
held at the Ian Potter Centre, Melbourne*

The spirits stand in their places
laced to the floor by cables,
a concentration of the strange;
the most real among halls of steel
and glass; ephemeral and unknown.
Pillars as solid as the trunks of trees
that gave them their bodies,
alive as the forests and open skies
they have left to stand guard here
beside the door to this gallery café

where strangers unwrap sandwiches,
know nothing of the other portal
beside their tables. I grieve
and grieve, whisper a greeting
to these tall dignified divinities
and tell them that moss still grows,
that the wind outside still sings.
They know how to wait in silence.

They listen to their country
which is here and no longer here.
I resist the impulse to cross
my chest, my heart held
under my tongue. I cannot ask
these muted guardians for blessings.
I cannot even pronounce their names.

Do they forgive the people
who were created by these spirits,
who carved their images,
for giving them up to strangers?
Forgive us for worse?
I cannot hear an answer.

The Plane Tree

The flesh of your roots
pours over stone and street,
bound as we are bound
by this relentless age.

We have tightened a belt
around your generous body,
corseted your ample waist.
Asphalt suffocates the soil
that nourishes your life.

The earth is not open
so you have forced it open:
given an inadequate square
you have rolled like water,
claiming a larger portion
of sunlight, defining curves
in place of straight lines,
a spilled puddle over edges.

Soft leaves shuffle above
in the shadowed air
as water and wood
make love in the gutter,
their meeting overcoming
the protestations of stone.

If I could take back
what soft warm humans
have said to trees
in such cold concrete terms —
I would roll away the street
and speak again with praise.
I would offer you only awe
for your liquidity and strength.

Forest/ry

At the periphery of vision
one might mistake these trees
for forest. *Better than pines*, we say,
as we drive through foothills like a dream
where movement brings no progress.

The inevitable sameness of monoculture
rolls along beside us. The trees too close,
too identical, too tall in their drawn-out
upward stretch to become timber for our use.

They seem half-alive, so spare of foliage,
already poles waiting to be felled. They repeat
the mantra we've all been taught: *economy
furniture bills schoolbooks economy economy* —

I want the old language back.
Looking for places it still speaks itself,
we drive towards a refuge of forgotten cadences,
a forest reserve deep in hardwood country.

Reserved but not original,
this sliver was allowed to regrow,
to stand for the land before the logging,
before this relentless economy.

It says *tree bird snake
lizard frog spider insect
moss mushroom mammal
seed sprout grow rot
water air sun soil.*
It says
*life
life
life.*

Mooloort Plains, 42°

All I can hear is heat.

No other voice dares to rise
and risk attention from this tyrant sun —
the terrible smothering affection
of the giver of life, this god of fire.

Even the bitumen yields,
offers up its hardness,
becomes a mirage that melts
an uncertain horizon.

The car protests, and we stop
beside a single file of roadside gums
spared the hunger of the crop —
last lonely remnants of shade.

The world, wide here to the edge,
has been reduced to a dry sea of grain
upon grain, a wound of land
bared and naked to the raging sky:

the hand that feeds us
is fast around our necks.

Big Plans for Baringhup

The plans for the broiler factory,
sewn as scrap of yellow on a fence,
have begun to spread — a rash
learning to turn the host's own cells
against itself. Residents are divided.
Post-holes pock the scarred ground,
already sick of over-grazing, worn out
like an old, stark-ribbed horse.

This high place was once a refuge,
a watershed now claimed for sheds
the size of footy ovals, to trap in
one million sorry chickens.
Before the factory, before the farms,
there were oases here.
Pooled miracles of swamp
rested improbably near the sky
for single seasons, moving
across the plains, waiting
for a wet spring to hold them down.

Dry air now rips away the topsoil
and rattles the barbed-wire boundary.
This rash, this sore that spreads,
itches under my skin
and I cannot reach to scratch.
Our letters are paper-thin hope

blown against the gold
of those old boys
that cooked this scheme.

These words too,
an insubstantial breath
that carries prayer to power,
while steel cages
already lure their crazed prisoners —
this gulag an end-product
of four thousand years of fences,
built to keep the jungle out
and the jungle birds in.

The Boys' Club
for Ann de Hugard

I love the smell of the boys' club,
all musty leather and dust
sifted down through the generations.
There's an armchair by the fire
where women can bring them cognac
to help distil their great thoughts.
To be sure, they value intelligent wives,
to listen and inform their work
without demanding any due.

I am indebted to those old boys.
I fell in love with at least ten dead men,
and their rule books make excellent platforms
from which to leap
into the unruly sea of the heart.
Some of their wisdom I more or less keep,
like where to put a semicolon;
reading suggestions from their canon;
and occasionally lovely shapes for verse.
Some days my bright threads
seem to love their solid loom.

Oh how I would like my own chair by the fire
and a matching handsome cup-bearer…

...though on second thoughts
I love to splash in puddles
and to lick my sticky fingers
in a warm chaotic kitchen.
I wouldn't want too much respectability
crowding in on my womanhood.
So I'll read their classic books
and learn how to write a sonnet

but they can't teach me how to dream
or tell me how to sing of them.

The Dishes

Constant as the need to eat.
As close to my life as the water in my blood,
the rush and gush from a turned tap,
heat pooling around hands
changed and aged by decades of women's work.

My years have taught me
that vaginas are precursors to housework:
a child of my tribe, I never saw my father clean.
He, the Alpha Male, away all day,
came home in the evening
to be served at the long table by the Alpha She.
My brother, the Beta,
didn't do anything useful as far as I could see,
except to keep the smile on our faces
in answer to his easy grin.
My younger sister cleared away the plates —
and I washed up.

This last shift was always mine,
after the dark and before bed.
I learned the pattern:
scrape, rinse, stack, plug, fill
(as hot as I could handle to speed the work),
squirt soap, scrub, rinse, stack.
For years I fought the pots,
steel wool a weapon against patches
of burned and dry, scratching the bottom.

Later, in my own kitchens,
I learned to soak, and wait,
to let the water do its slow work.
I learned that there is grace to be found,
there in the humble repetition of a simple task,
in the solitude of quiet thoughts
over a sink at day's end,
a peace when the fight goes out
and a sweet acceptance takes its place.
I began to love the neat stack,
the satisfaction when all is drying on the rack.
This small ritual of renewal can be a balm
for a heart not so easily cleaned.

And I found a sisterhood,
this shared experience of generations,
each of us alone with a task
we'd really rather not do.
The way, after a meal,
some lean back into their chairs
and others lean forward to clear the plates,
to wipe clean the table
with curving circles of a damp cloth.
The way, at parties,
a bustle of women collects in the kitchen,
taking turns to wash and dry, chat and fuss,
return serving plates and containers
into their owner's care.

When I left home at seventeen,
my parents bought a dishwasher,
replacing me with a machine.
I lived for a year with two women.
In solidarity, we unclamped the hoses
of the robot in our kitchen,
dragged it to the shed.
We would not burn coal to do
what our hands knew so well,
and for the first time in our lives
did no more than our share.

Later, in a sprawling chaotic share-house,
I surrendered to a dishwasher;
patiently explained to housemates
(whose mothers and sisters had sheltered
from the mysteries of housework)
that dishes need scraping and rinsing by hand
before being shoved into its maw.

For now, I live alone in a quiet house,
cooking simple meals for one;
find a calm in the old familiar task
to contrast each day's novel convolutions.

So much of my future will be flux,
so much of it hidden from me here —
but I know this constant waits:
the pooled water, my knowing hands,
the use and renewal of a lifetime's dishes.

An Armful

I.

The shapes of things we carry
worry at our outlines,
as the sea piles sand around a curve of beach;
as our hands are worn by what we hold.
We wrap our selves around us,
keep close our secret lives,
each afraid — were we to let them go —
the flesh remaining might collapse,
reduced to flaccid belly or stubby toe.

Like Atlas, we balance on our backs
entire worlds, and step the line
that strings the span from birth
all the way to uncertainty,
knowing that at any moment
we could fall into the void
of our disgrace.

II.

And so my arms arc this holding pose,
filled with memories of sunshine
and that old fear of falling.
The curl of fingers throws shadows
on the water that waits beneath:
they shape a wolf, perhaps,
or the beak of a bird
to pluck mysteries or revelations
from the swarming sea.

I tiptoe on the wire,
sometimes slipping,
accustomed to my burden of loving
and curious leftover bits of life;
while the ocean in my heart
yields enough pearls to sustain me.

I doubt I will ever release the sea
or radically reshape the shore
though my toes still edge along
and I wobble and sway
in an awkward dance
that might just turn out
to be grace.

Hungry Ghost

This body is the ghost that haunts my sleep:
the dreaming soul untroubled by demands
as tug the questing belly and its hungry host.

The quiet spirit offers quiet rest
to raging flesh that bleeds and sweats.

Hands wring their distress, command a use.
Feet itch to obey their restive function
while the heart insists on leaping sideways
towards its prey. The traitor brain conspires:
greedy for control of this unruly fray.

In silence, spirit offers silent rest
to restless flesh that needs and frets.

Who Down on the Heart's Rug

Who down on the heart's rug can rise
to set a tinder burning in the grate?
Fingers too cold to pinch a match,
the hearth only slabs of hard slate,
a bed of dust and ash piled thick
where love's fire should be dancing.

When the worn heel folds under foot,
any movement seems a journey
to the burnt end of life's embers.
The fireplace waits for a hand
to bring up heat from ashes,
for the slumping body to stand.

I Will not Fall Again

I will not fall from love again
I will not fall from love
I will not fall
I will not

Fever Dream

In a world of green
newborn spring,
red-hot life-heat rages,
swelling into buds.

Outside, a chill wind cuts
underneath the warm sun;
inside, I am cold, deep
in the clutches of fever,

on the edge of not-quite sleep,
trying to recall
the patience of mushrooms
growing in the dark.

I scrawl sweat on red sheets.
The curtains are framed
in lurid light; too bright
against the dim room.

Into the void of dreams
a terror comes;
snaking into vision
more real than life.

Plunging, swimming
in congealed darkness,
in the almost-red light
behind my eyelids,

I am moving nightmare-slow;
pursued now
by a serpent goddess,
her jaws snapping at my feet.

We are submerged in
the convolutions of flesh,
in red of every shade,
all liquid — no air —

though
impossibly
She
is fire.

In terror, I seek escape,
flail my body
in a refueled attempt
at propulsion.

She, effortless,
undulates
inexorably
closer.

In the moment
that I know she must
consume me, know
there is no sense in flight,

I know her name:
Kali
destroyer,
burner, cleanser;

her fertile heat still
pulsing
unmistakably
towards mine.

In the moment
she devours me
I am gone;
the flesh is gone.

Now there is only
a snake in the void;
and now,
only the void.

The flames have fed,
are sated and silent.
Kali is elsewhere,
picking her teeth.

Elemental

I.

If you were water
I would tell you
your nature is to fall

If you were air
I would suck you in
knowing lungs
can only hold so much

If you were earth
I would plant myself as seed
only to crack open inside you
hungry for the sky

If you were fire
I would burn to ash
to feed your appetite

II.

To feed your appetite
I would plant myself as seed

I would burn to ash
only to crack open inside you

I would suck you in
hungry for the sky

Knowing lungs
can only hold so much
I would tell you
your nature is to fall

Collier's Lilith

Such wealth of hair, so soft
to the mind's fingers, skin
warm enough to urge us
to transgression, to drink
too much of such goodness.

Standing before shadows,
draped in a light that paints
an undress of unhidden self,
clothed only in a single loving
arm of snake that curves
to wrap her bright body
in its silky grip, while
her radiance distracts
the eye away from depths
of darkness behind her.

A heat of blood poured
through pulse and brush
to give us this image
of our desire, of our divinity.
We are filled by a rush
of wanting, moving, having;
calm in stillness, she rests
like a mirror to our chase.

The Poem

I walk around my house,
looking for a poem,
ready for it to edge
out from behind my dead
confined in their frames.
I promise to meet it kindly
when it comes.

I walk around my house
and realise it is not my house.

I ask each room
until the house tells me
it belongs only to itself.
The dead speak, tell me
they will keep poetry hidden
behind their frames, until I admit
the poems belong only to themselves.

Now I walk around this house
looking for something that is mine.
Each thing I touch tells me
it belongs to itself.

I find a mirror,
look at the shape it shows me
and realise it is not my body.
It belongs to itself.

My eyes watch me
watching them.
Is this the poem?
Is this my self?

Strangers in the Dark

Close the senses, lower lids,
so some dream may sidle in,
stepped off a night-train on travels
who knows from where;
let it lift clean the blanket of sleep
to lie with the mind, all open
and warm, and kiss its brow,
bringing to grow inside the hard case
a soft thing.

Waiting like Eros
for a blind moment after the candle,
the giver, by nature unseen,
slips beside us in our beds
and delivers its mystery, encrypted
in shape-shifted story and picture,
deep into the bellies of our brains.

We open every time,
allow the ocean of dream
to pour into the world beneath:
we who worship gods of order
and common tactile sense
can forget these night stars by day
but they stay, are seeds
that raise shoots into thought.

The side that shows conceals
the face of our far-sided moon:
we who long for reason's light
love as truly these strangers
who come to us in the dark;
are lovers of dream's unbidden gifts

unless they bite.

Time and Eternity
after A. K. Coomeraswamy

she who desires
knowledge sits at a window
looking out towards a beginning
outside time
binding the whole in a net
consummation of moments
equal to zero
mass making space
both at once and everywhere
she looks from a moving car
to a mountain that seems to stay still
dancing on the edge of being
motionless at the centre
.

Panta Rhei
after Heracleitus

This

stained-glass reality
lets in the light
that loves to bounce,
bend, glance from eye

to gleaming eye —
all colour, art,
each leaf and curl
of line to plane

and curve of shell
a mirror game
to marvel, play,
revel in the light

then bend its back
to shadow, black
and dark. So we
might turn away;

die, submerge,
return to day
somehow changed
and changed again,

so never twice the same;
not for one moment
allowed to pause
an image or a sound,

though marble
may wait our gaze
and seem to promise
stillness — still

we must move on,
the statue will
in time, time, time
crumble at last

long past our own
decay. *Panta Rhei*
the law remains,
all things flow —

and only their source
at the centre stays.

www.ingramcontent.com/pod-product-compliance
Lightning Source LLC
Chambersburg PA
CBHW030458010526
44118CB00011B/991